DATE DUE

TECH GIRLS

Careers for

TECH GIRLS IN TECHNOLOGY

CAROL HAND

ROSEN PUBLISHING®

New York

Published in 2016 by The Rosen Publishing Group, Inc.
29 East 21st Street, New York, NY 10010

Copyright © 2016 by The Rosen Publishing Group, Inc.

First Edition

Library of Congress Cataloging-in-Publication Data

Hand, Carol, 1945–
Careers for tech girls in technology/Carol Hand.—First edition.
      pages cm.—(Tech girls)
Includes bibliographical references and index.
ISBN 978-1-4994-6099-5 (library bound)
1. Technology—Vocational guidance—Juvenile literature.
2. Women in engineering—Juvenile literature. I. Title.
TA157.5.H35 2016
602.3—dc23
                                                                        2014044519

Manufactured in the United States of America

CONTENTS

errie Cobb flew her first airplane at age twelve. At age twenty-eight, she was a record-breaking pilot. She had broken the world altitude record and the world speed record for light planes. She had ferried fighter jets around the world, transporting them to war zones. She had logged more than 7,000 flying hours—compared to 5,000 for John Glenn and 2,900 for Scott Carpenter, two of NASA's seven Mercury astronauts. Cobb would have been thrilled to become an astronaut, but in 1959, women were not only barred from being astronauts, they were also barred from the only position that would qualify them to be considered—that of military test pilot. Female pilots had trouble getting any meaningful flying jobs. Few qualified women were allowed to fly passengers—they were told no one would fly with a female pilot. Many settled for being cargo transporters or crop dusters. Others flew smaller planes than they were qualified for or became flight instructors.

Early in the space program, NASA refused to consider women as astronaut candidates. When a letter that suggested enrolling female astronauts crossed his desk, Vice President Lyndon B. Johnson wrote across the letter, "Let's Stop This Now!" Alan Shepard and Deke Slayton, two of the original Mercury 7 astronauts, wrote a book in which they described the qualities required to be an astronaut. They ended their description with the words, "…and, of course, no women, thank you."

εηφυειω 8388329929 φδφ ΗΓΗΓΔΥΨΕΘΚΙΛ

ΔΘΩ : κδιε # 3448

ΔΥΟ : δφιχ # 7837

ΙΦΒ : νϖσι # 9832

Jerrie Cobb views a rocket display at a 1961 space conference. Cobb was denied the chance to become an astronaut, but her tireless lobbying efforts paved the way for other women to come.

But one man was not bound by such prejudice. Dr. Randolph Lovelace was the chairman of NASA's Life Sciences Committee and a designer of the medical tests taken by all astronaut candidates. He took a practical approach. He reasoned that because women, on average, had an anatomically smaller and lighter build than men, they would fit more easily into cramped spacecraft, use less oxygen, and require less fuel to achieve orbit. Lovelace also thought women had the necessary physical and psychological toughness. Nevertheless, he understood that he would meet resistance and need proof. His friend Donald Flickinger, a U.S. Air Force general and NASA adviser, had air force funds and agreed to sponsor astronaut tests on women. Jerrie Cobb was their first candidate. The air force shot down the idea before Cobb could even begin.

Undeterred, Lovelace tested Cobb in secret. In February 1960, she completed all eighty-seven physical and psychological tests taken by astronaut candidates. She passed them all. Lovelace identified eighteen more candidates, and in 1961, he ran them through the same tests. Thirteen women passed. Several, including Cobb, equaled or exceeded the scores of successful male candidates. Doctors furthermore commented that the women complained much less about the tests than the men had. Lovelace arranged to do the second phase of testing at a naval facility in Pensacola, Florida. Cobb completed the tests in May 1961 and again passed with flying colors. Then, the navy—informed officially by NASA that no program for female astronauts existed—refused to proceed. Tests on the other women were cancelled, and the thirteen women never became astronauts.

Although Cobb and others lobbied tirelessly, nothing happened until 1978, when the United States finally began to recruit women astronauts. In June 1983, Sally Ride became the first U.S. woman in space. In 1995, Eileen Collins became the first woman to pilot a space shuttle, and in June 1999, Collins commanded STS-93—becoming the first woman to command a space shuttle. Attending the launch, at Collins's invitation, were Jerrie Cobb and seven of the original "Mercury 13"—the "almost astronauts." Although these women never made it into the astronaut program, their daring and determination helped pave the way for today's female astronauts—and for women in all technology careers.

Chapter one

THE T IN STEM: WHAT ARE TECHNOLOGY CAREERS?

STEM careers are those that involve the fields of science, technology, engineering, and math. People pursuing STEM careers give us a cutting-edge society, with new and exciting inventions and changes. They make our lives easier and push us forward into the future.

Technology careers are one of four types of STEM careers. Technology is the "application of knowledge to the practical aims of human life or to changing and manipulating the human environment." More simply, it is the practical application of knowledge. Technology has been around since people began using tools. It began as a way to replace human or animal labor with machines. Over the centuries, tools have become more and more complex. Technology is now an essential part of our culture.

WHAT ARE STEM CAREERS?

Careers in science, technology, engineering, and mathematics often overlap, but they have slightly different aims or objectives. Science and mathematics are considered "pure" areas of knowledge; they deal with problems that—at least at first—have no practical value or "real-world" application. People tackle these problems because the problems are interesting and because they want to understand better how the world works. Engineering and technology, in contrast,

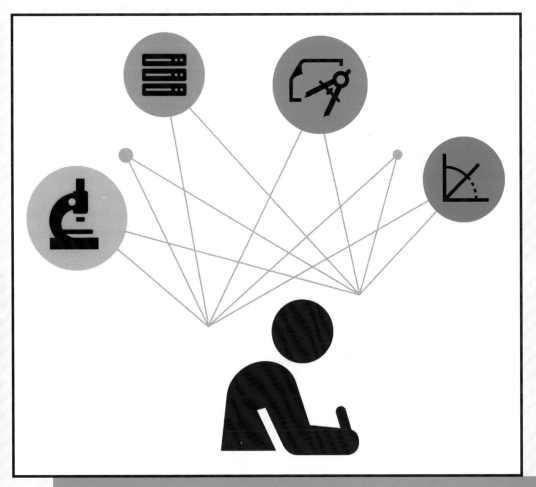

Careers in STEM (science, technology, engineering, and mathematics) fields are interrelated and often overlap. A solid understanding of concepts in math and science is essential for any STEM career.

focus on practical applications; they are forms of "applied" science. Applied scientists use known scientific concepts to solve specific problems. Engineers use scientific principles to design structures, equipment, or materials. They may design computers, buildings, medicines, or spacecraft. If the problem is getting from one side of a river to the other, engineers design a bridge. Technologists use the structures, equipment, or materials designed by engineers. They build structures such as bridges. They assemble and

INVENTOR AS TECHNOLOGIST

Alabama-born Mary Anderson was visiting New York City in 1903. During a rainstorm, she noticed that streetcar drivers had to open their windows and stick their heads out to see the street clearly. Anderson saw a problem, and she decided to solve it. She invented a swinging metal arm with a rubber blade that attached to the outside of the car. Drivers could operate it from inside their vehicle by using a lever. She called it the "windshield wiper." By 1916, it was standard equipment on most vehicles. In 1917, another woman, Charlotte Bridgwood, improved Anderson's invention by making the windshield wiper automatic. Inventors such as Anderson and Bridgwood illustrate technology at its best—applying science to solve problems.

install equipment, run it, maintain and repair it, or otherwise integrate it into our technological society.

Inevitably, someone quickly figures out practical applications for discoveries in basic science. To make an application usable, people from all four STEM areas often work together. Before an engineer can design a spacecraft, or a technologist can launch it, both must understand the principles of mathematics and physics that make space flight possible. The genetic engineering of a new plant species requires scientists, including geneticists and biochemists. Scientists with mathematical skills determine required DNA manipulations. Technologists carry out laboratory techniques to cut and splice the DNA and to produce and grow the new organism.

A STEM OVERVIEW

An online search for technology careers often yields lists of job titles suggesting that technology is equivalent to computer science. In one article, nine of eleven jobs listed as "best technology jobs" are in information technology (IT); they include web developer, computer systems analyst, and computer support specialist. Nearly all tech careers require an understanding of computers, the Internet, and computer control of systems. However, computer use is often just a means to an end. The ultimate goal might be long-distance control of a satellite or robot, or analysis of the function of a medical implant.

Technology jobs exist in any field that uses machines—and that is nearly every field. A person interested in transportation might go into automotive

More and more women are entering green technology and engineering careers. One green career is the building of solar, or photovoltaic, energy farms such as this one.

technology, working on engines for gas, diesel, electric, or hybrid vehicles. Collision repair, truck and heavy equipment repair, and use of computerized diagnostic equipment are other transportation-related careers. Electrical power plants must be operated and maintained by highly skilled technologists who specialize in specific power sources—for example, fossil fuels, hydropower, nuclear energy, or solar or wind power.

Many construction careers use technology. These include basic construction careers, such as framing, carpentry, or plumbing. Construction technicians may specialize in construction management, drafting, or inspection technology and typically work under engineers. Technologists are also vital in manufacturing. Recently, both automation and demand for precision have increased in manufacturing. Manufacturing technicians maintain and repair production equipment that keeps the manufacturing process running smoothly.

BECOMING A TECHNOLOGIST

Early preparation for careers in all four STEM areas is the same. A girl in middle or high school should take all available courses in science, mathematics, and computer science, plus any specialized courses in technology and engineering. She should become comfortable using computers, tablets, and other electronic devices. This means more than typing in assignments, conducting Google searches, and texting friends. She should become comfortable using basic software, such as word processors, spreadsheets, and graphics programs. Extracurricular activities are important, too. Technology clubs, science fairs and contests, and technological hobbies (building a robot or solar car, designing a method to prevent pollution, or inventing a new medical device) can immerse girls early into the world of technology.

Girls in high school and college should also look for summer jobs or internships in STEM areas. They should find a mentor—a woman who has "made it" in a technology field and who can provide advice on how to succeed in a STEM career. Finally, they should apply for grants and scholarships especially for women. Most important, they should not close any doors! Before and during college, girls should prepare for any potential technology career by getting a thorough education and taking advantage of the best extracurricular opportunities available.

CAN GIRLS BE TECHNOLOGISTS?

The short answer is: of course they can! This is an excellent time for girls and women to enter technology fields because people now realize women are underrepresented in many STEM careers, and many companies are actively seeking female employees. Women in the United States hold 57 percent of all bachelor's degrees and more than 60 percent of master's degrees—triple the number in 1970. More than half of all women (57.7 percent) are in the workforce. However, women's participation in most STEM careers is much lower than their participation in, for example, the fields of teaching, psychology, and public relations. Only 22 percent of environmental scientists and 17 percent of chemical engineers are women. Some engineering fields have as few as 5.5 percent women. Very few women currently follow technology careers relating to "hard" sciences such as physics. Many more go into "soft" sciences such as biology. For example, 46 percent of biological scientists, 78 percent of clinical laboratory technicians, and 91 percent of nurses are women.

Should girls limit themselves to career paths in which women are already strongly represented— nursing or laboratory technicians, for example? Definitely not! Every girl should follow her passion. A girl who loves tinkering with engines might aim for a career as an airplane mechanic. If running electronic equipment for a television studio excites her,

A college degree is the first step toward most technology careers. Women are especially needed in what are called "hard sciences," such as physics, engineering, and computer technology.

she should go for it! If she wants to, she should get her hands dirty working with sanitation equipment designed to reduce waste. Such jobs are both necessary and increasingly important. In short, any girl or woman can strive for—and achieve—any technology career goal that appeals to her. Women will be a large part of the solution for many of today's (and tomorrow's) technological problems.

Chapter two

COMMUNICATION TECHNOLOGY: CHATTING 'ROUND THE WORLD

*A*nyone who has watched a movie or television and thought, "Wow, that's a great camera angle!" or, "How exactly do satellites transfer images halfway around the world?" has the mind-set of a communication technologist. Anyone whose friends call her to troubleshoot their software problems is already using her communication technology abilities. The person who installs equipment and software to run a cell tower is a technologist. The person who sets up a sound system for a media performance is a technologist. So is the Geek Squad member who, with a few deft keystrokes, brings a dead computer back to life. Careers in communication technology are almost endless and should only improve in the future.

According to the organization QFINANCE, "Communication technology facilitates communication between individuals or groups who are not physically present at the same location. Systems such as telephones, telex, fax, radio, television, and video are included, as well as more recent computer-based technologies, including electronic data interchange and e-mail." Communication technology is also called telecommunications, or telecom. Information technology (IT) deals specifically with the functions and abilities of computers. Because most modern communication uses digital data transfer—that is, computers—the two technologies overlap considerably.

MEDIA COMMUNICATION JOBS

Many people working in media (radio, television, film, and electronic media) have careers in the spotlight, for example, as actors or news anchors. However,

Being a camerawoman in television, film, or video production is an exciting technology career. Camera operators must be creative, visual, and technical experts—they must know camera equipment plus editing software.

those most skilled in technology often work behind the scenes, as broadcast technicians, camera operators, directors, producers, or animators. These people make sure the show goes on without a hitch. Others work in publishing of print or electronic media. Communication technologists find careers in publication houses, television studios, radio stations, or corporate media departments. They might specialize in news, sports, entertainment, education, science, or business. Most people in writing-based careers—authors, bloggers,

CAREERS IN MEDIA COMMUNICATION TECHNOLOGY

Communication technology careers are not limited to television, movies, and the Internet. Nearly all companies employ technologists in careers such as the following:

- Audio and video equipment technicians
- Broadcast technicians
- Camera operators
- Camera and photographic equipment repairers
- Desktop publishers
- Film and video editors
- Graphic designers
- Multimedia artists and animators
- Sound engineering technicians
- Station programmers

copywriters, and reporters, for example—use communication technology as a major tool.

WORLDWIDE TELECOMMUNICATIONS JOBS

Telecommunication carries digital information around the world, and the jobs associated with this technology are exciting and varied. Telecommunication careers include the people who provide services such as high-speed Internet, wireless communication, and cable television. They may install, maintain, or repair equipment supplying such services. Typical jobs include network systems analyst, data communication analyst, and communication equipment operator.

A key feature of the telecom industry is rapid change. Since the Telecom Act of 1996, boundaries between various providers have blurred. Before this legislation, each type of telecommunication was provided separately. The Telecom Act of 1996 made it legal for a single firm to offer local, long-distance, wireless, and Internet services. As technology advances, future technologists must be able to adapt quickly and fearlessly to changes and constantly learn new technologies. They must know the products and be able to speak the correct technical jargon. Often, a technologist will specialize in one particular aspect—for example, fiber optics or wireless technology—but a general knowledge of the entire field is essential. While many people in the telecom field will do fieldwork—such as installing and repairing telecom systems, for example—others may work in office jobs such as network planning, equipment sales, or management. These areas require less specific technological knowledge, but they do require a strong general understanding of the field.

SERVICE-RELATED COMMUNICATION JOBS

A little recognized field in communication technology is the customer support staff. These technicians answer telephone calls or e-mails when people have questions about their computers or other electronic devices. They answer questions and talk callers step-by-step through simple fixes. They make house calls

The customer support representative who fields calls when someone's computer crashes must be an expert at fixing computers, sight unseen. She must also be polite, friendly, and helpful.

when cable or satellite service goes out. They work behind the service desk at electronics stores to set up or repair individuals' computers or printers.

Customer service technicians need both excellent communication skills and technical know-how. Because they work directly with the public, they must always project a pleasant, helpful attitude. According to the American Management Association, when a company loses business, 68 percent of the time it is because of poor customer service—usually because the service representative is either rude or indifferent. Patience, good listening skills, simple and accurate communication, and knowledge of products are among the many skills required of a customer service representative. Their salaries do not necessarily match those of other careers in the technology sector, but customer service representatives are an indispensable part of the telecommunications industry.

PREPARING FOR COMMUNICATION TECHNOLOGY JOBS

Girls interested in communication technology careers can obtain valuable experience before college by seeking out activities related to their field of interest. Someone interested in an entertainment or media career might join a theater or musical group or work on a stage crew. Someone interested in news, publications, or electronic media might intern at a radio or television station, at a web venture, or for a newspaper. One planning to go into a customer service career in the technology sector might seek a job at a

TELECOM ORGANIZATIONS FOR GIRLS AND WOMEN

Many organizations provide information and mentoring for girls and women interested in careers in information and communication technology. Some of those organizations include:

- The Association for Women in Technology (AWT): http://www.awtsocal.org
- Braincake Girls, Math and Science Partnership, Carnegie Science Centre Program: http://www.braincake.org/whoweare.aspx
- Canadian Coalition of Women in Engineering, Science, Trades, and Technology: http://www.ccwestt.org
- Feminist Approach to Technology (FAT): http://www.fat-net.org/content/about-us
- Girls Excelling in Math and Science (GEMS) clubs: http://www.gemsclub.org/index.html
- Girls in ICT: http://girlsinict.org/trends-analysis-and-profiles
- Girls in Tech (GIT): http://www.girlsintech.org
- MentorNet: http://www.mentornet.net
- The Wired Woman: http://www.thewiredwoman.com
- Women in Cable Telecommunications (WICT): http://www.wict.org/about/Pages/default.aspx

local electronics store and help friends and neighbors with their electronics problems.

Education for telecom careers varies. On-the-job training through internships, apprenticeships, or entry-level jobs might be sufficient for customer service technicians, but many people obtain bachelor's degrees in communications with an emphasis on digital film or motion picture production. A broadcast and sound engineering technician typically needs either an associate's degree or a non-degreed training course. Film and video editors and camera operators usually require a bachelor's degree in audio and video technology and film. This would also qualify the holder to sell, install, operate, or repair audio-visual equipment. People interested in news production usually obtain a degree in journalism and broadcasting. This qualifies them to research, write, and produce news stories, as well as install, operate, and repair the digital and electronic equipment used in news production.

Anyone seeking a career involving installation, repair, replacement, or operation of electrical or electronic equipment will need an associate's degree from a technical college. Obtaining certification, in addition to a degree, is helpful in landing a job. Because digital communication is so widespread, people with this kind of training can work in telecommunications, transportation, or utilities, or find a relevant job in almost any industry.

WOMEN IN COMMUNICATION TECHNOLOGY

Currently, women account for about 25 percent of information and communication technology (ICT) workers in Europe and about 20 percent in the United States. Women also make up most of the low-paying, temporary workers in the field, while men occupy the most of the high-level "knowledge worker" positions.

Vice President Joe Biden speaks at Renton Technical College in Renton, Washington, in 2014. Federal government funding supports technical colleges such as Renton, which train much-needed technologists.

Some women may be intimidated by the requirements for these careers or by working in often male-dominated fields.

But times are changing, and the upcoming generation can help make this change happen. Women are recognizing the employment gap and beginning to seek out these careers. Technology scholarships are becoming increasingly available for women, and helpful groups are springing up to aid and encourage women who want to enter telecommunications careers. It is likely that the percentage of girls and women in telecommunications will continue to rise in the coming years.

AEROSPACE AND DEFENSE TECHNOLOGY: TO EXPLORE AND PROTECT

The aerospace and defense industries are exciting fields for girls and women. The technologies of these two industries are similar, but not all aerospace technologies have military applications. After the fall of communism in 1989 and the subsequent end of the Cold War, the U.S. government began research projects to develop civilian uses for defense technologies, and defense companies expanded into commercial markets. Thus, an aerospace technologist might help produce a satellite or support the next mission to the International Space Station (ISS). One of NASA's specific goals is to develop one non-aerospace or non-defense application for each new technology that it produces.

AN ARRAY OF CAREERS

The vast array of careers available in aerospace and defense enables technology specialists to work with commercial or private jets; spy, weather, or communication satellites; flight simulators; submarines; aircraft

SECTORS IN AEROSPACE AND DEFENSE TECHNOLOGY

According to the website Military.com, the military and aerospace industry builds and services various types of equipment:

- Commercial (non-military) airplanes and helicopters
- Military aircraft such as the F-15 Eagle and F-117 Stealth Fighter
- Missiles and components for the International Space Station
- Armored vehicles, such as the M1 Abrams tank
- Satellite-based technologies that are used for weather forecasting; traffic control and GPS systems; worldwide communications; infrared, radar, and sonar technologies; avionics and missile-guidance systems; and information systems such as NASA's Mission Control
- Aircraft carriers, destroyers, and submarines

Small armies of highly trained technologists and technicians operate, maintain, and repair all this equipment.

carriers; missiles; or tanks and munitions. Many of the largest firms that manufacture these technologies—Lockheed Martin, Boeing, and Raytheon—are based in the United States. There are also hundreds of smaller companies that manufacture the thousands of smaller pieces required to put together a jet or a satellite. All these companies are potential employers for tomorrow's aerospace and defense technologists.

Aerospace and defense is a massive industry that employs perhaps more technologists than any

In 2014, approximately 1,100 working satellites orbited Earth, working in telecommunications, broadcast, weather observations, national defense, science, and agriculture. Technologists monitor these satellites.

other. Some participants in this field will work on cutting-edge technologies that are decades ahead of those available to the public. One of the greatest expansions has been in the area of satellite communications. However, many companies—particularly the very large ones—change slowly. While a segment of aerospace and defense workers develop incredibly advanced technology, much of the technology still in use was introduced in the 1970s and 1980s. Technology development is extremely expensive, and if a technology works, there is little need or incentive to change it. Thus, a woman hoping to enter the field should consider whether she wants to work on cutting-edge or tried-and-true technologies and then focus her efforts in the right area.

THE FUTURE OF SPACE TECHNOLOGY

Much of the next generation of space technology may happen in private industry. NASA's space shuttle program ended in 2011 after thirty years, leaving NASA without a space-going vehicle. The California-based space transport services company SpaceX is filling that vacuum. SpaceX has developed both the Falcon rocket and the Dragon spacecraft. The

On March 1, 2013, a SpaceX Falcon 9 rocket launched from Cape Canaveral, Florida, carrying supplies to the International Space Station. There are plans for SpaceX rockets to someday carry people into space.

ALYSSA CARSON, FUTURE ASTRONAUT

Alyssa Carson, of Baton Rouge, Louisiana, is thirteen years old, and her goal is to be the first person on Mars. In an October 2014 profile by NPR, Alyssa said, "I want to go to Mars because it's a place no one has been. It's completely deserted right now. So I want to take that first step." According to NASA spokesman Paul Foreman, "She is doing the right things, taking the right training, following the right steps to actually become an astronaut." At the time of her interview, Alyssa had already attended all three of NASA's world space camps and was studying science, math, and several foreign languages. She declared, "Failure is not an option."

Dragon, which is launched with the aid of the Falcon rocket, has already delivered cargo to the International Space Station.

The ultimate goal of SpaceX is to carry people to the moon and to Mars. To that end, the company is currently refining the Falcon and the Dragon for human passengers. Projects such as this mean that space technology companies are always seeking the top talent in the technology sector to build new vehicles and equipment. Expert technologists are needed to build rockets, spacecraft, and propulsion systems; to launch, test, and fly vehicles; and to carry out quality control tests and procedures that ensure the safest possible vehicles. Girls excited about space may find careers at SpaceX, other private space contractors, or NASA, which plans to send humans to Mars by 2025. Skilled technologists may find space-related opportunities working as communications specialists, electricians, laser technicians, radar technicians, robotic technicians, or satellite technologists. Determined ones may end up using their skills in space.

CAREERS IN THE MILITARY

One way to enter the aerospace and defense industry is by joining the military. Enlisted military members do not need college training. After basic training, they undertake Advanced Individual Training (AIT) to learn specific skills. Each military branch offers its own set of career fields, many of them technology-related. For example, army recruits in the Air Defense Artillery School learn about high-tech missile systems. Those in the Transportation School learn to operate and maintain army trucks, material-handling equipment, and watercraft. Each military branch has similar training schools. Enlisted recruits can earn college credits while developing skills for their military career. Many young people join the military partly because of its educational benefits.

Officers are military leaders involved in decision making, planning, organizing, and directing operations. They must complete a four-year college degree before entering the military and then complete Officer Candidate School (OCS). All marine officer candidates complete training in a Military Occupational Specialty (MOS) and serve as leaders within this specialty. Many MOS areas—for example, intelligence,

A female marine works at Fox Camp, a marine logistics base in the desert of Kuwait. Women are vital to the military, and many military positions are technology oriented.

communications, and field artillery—have a strong technology orientation.

WOMEN IN THE MILITARY

In 2013, more than 200,000 women were enlisted in the military, compared to 40,000 in 1965. All combat jobs remained officially off-limits for women, but many women—including those serving as medics, military police, and intelligence officers—often found themselves in combat roles in places such as Afghanistan and Iraq. In 2013, defense secretary

A WOMAN IN COMBAT

In 2004, Cassandra Partee was stationed in Iraq. Partee had trained for combat artillery, but once in Iraq, she did whatever job was needed. She drove trucks and participated in house-to-house raids with combat patrols because the military wanted female officers present to search female Iraqis. At 1:00 AM, returning from an eleven-hour patrol, Partee saw something attached to a guardrail ahead. She had no choice except to proceed, so she stepped on the gas. A bomb went off, injuring both Partee and her commander. The two women had not been assigned to combat roles but still faced many of the dangers of combat. Partee received a Purple Heart for her injuries and is now a staff sergeant. She is pleased that the combat ban was lifted, but she says, "That is what I've known. It just seems normal to me."

Leon Panetta opened up more than 230,000 combat positions to women in the army and marines. A year later, there had been little progress in integrating women into the new jobs. According to Greg Jacob, a former marine and current policy director for Service Women's Action Network, job-testing procedures focus on strength-based measures rather than on the skills needed for each task. This focus often puts women at a disadvantage. In the time since, the army has worked on developing and improving gender-neutral standards for each army job, based on the skills and abilities needed for that specific job.

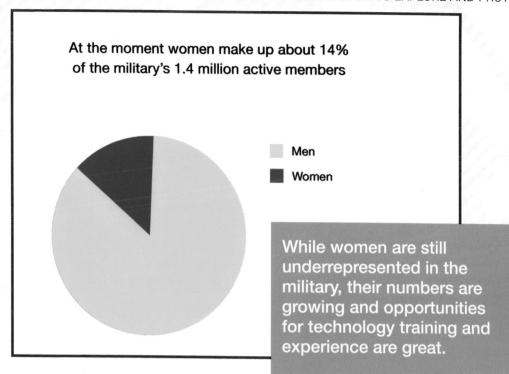

At the moment women make up about 14% of the military's 1.4 million active members

Men

Women

While women are still underrepresented in the military, their numbers are growing and opportunities for technology training and experience are great.

Historically, there have been sexual harassment problems in the military, just as in civilian life. Many of these issues continue today. Most offenders have been male coworkers in the same unit who held higher ranks than the complainant. The problem is real, and female military members should be aware of it. Cases of sexual harassment are often underreported, but any person who has suffered sexual harassment should report the incident to her commanding officer or another trusted official. Not all female soldiers suffer harassment or discrimination. Some have safe, positive experiences with their fellow unit members. Iraq veteran Cassandra Partee says, "There wasn't any discrimination. The majority of my battalion was male, but they didn't treat us any different." As for dealing with sexual harassment and assault, in March 2014 a

Department of Defense official stated, "We aren't leaving any options off the table to prevent sexual harassment." The D.O.D. plans to emphasize improvement of oversight and training, as well as strengthening procedures for managing sexual harassment incidents.

GETTING INTO AEROSPACE AND DEFENSE TECHNOLOGY

The education required for a career in aerospace and defense depends on the career. A military career will provide education and allow service members to continue their education after their service, paying the complete cost of education through graduate school. Jobs in the private sector, or in aerospace outside the military, usually require at least a bachelor's degree.

Some grants and scholarships in these areas are related to specific universities and are available for both men and women. For example, the Virginia Space Grant Consortium provides scholarships to students pursuing degrees at affiliated Virginia colleges. Similar scholarships are available in other states. NASA offers fellowships for undergraduate, graduate, and postgraduate students. It also has opportunities for high school and college summer programs and research studies. The Interdisciplinary National Science Project Incorporating Research and Education Experience (INSPIRE) is a year-round program targeting students in grades 9–12 with an interest in STEM careers. In INSPIRE's Online Learning Community (OLC), participants interact with likeminded students around the nation.

Chapter four

GREEN TECHNOLOGY: SAVING NATURE THROUGH TECHNOLOGY

The Bureau of Labor Statistics defines green jobs as jobs "that produce goods or provide services that benefit the environment or conserve natural resources," or that make "production processes more environmentally friendly or use fewer natural resources." Some technology jobs (for example, electricians) already exist but will require workers with more knowledge of environmental issues in the future. Other green careers are relatively new and will become increasingly important. These include such jobs as biomass plant technicians, climate change analysts, and geothermal technicians.

WHAT IS GREEN TECHNOLOGY?

Green technology, or environmental technology, refers to methods involved in living without destroying or damaging Earth, its organisms, or its ecosystems, and without overexploiting its resources. Major goals of green technology include

This BigBelly Solar Compactor, a trash compactor that runs on solar power, is an example of green technology. Its capacity is five times greater than a normal trash bin.

sustainability, "cradle-to-cradle" design, source reduction, innovation, and viability.

Sustainability means using resources to provide for this generation's needs without compromising the resources needed for coming generations. "Cradle-to-cradle" design involves manufacturing processes that enable every manufactured product to be completely reused or recycled, in contrast to our current "cradle-to-grave" or throwaway society. Source reduction involves decreasing waste and pollution by using fewer raw materials and producing less waste when producing and consuming

THE GREEN ECONOMY

The U.S. Department of Labor has identified twelve sectors of the economy that are sources of present and future green careers:

- Agriculture and forestry
- Energy and carbon capture
- Energy efficiency
- Energy trading
- Environmental protection
- Governmental and regulatory administration
- Green construction
- Manufacturing
- Recycling and waste reduction
- Renewable energy generation
- Research, design, and consulting services
- Transportation

manufactured items. Innovation and viability center around the development of alternatives to damaging technologies and the creation of economically viable products and careers that benefit the planet.

GREEN TECHNOLOGY CAREERS

Trends are converging to make environmental careers a key direction for women of the future. World energy consumption will increase by almost

50 percent between 2015 and 2035. Increased electrical demand will foster a need for new technologies to produce and transport energy efficiently. Rapid climate change will require people to search for new ways to reduce carbon emissions, including a transition from fossil fuels to renewable energy sources such as wind and solar energy. Finally, many current mining and manufacturing practices must become more environmentally friendly. In short, future green technologists must find creative methods of using resources that will also protect the environment.

Businesses around the country are adopting a "triple bottom line"—an accounting framework that emphasizes a balance of economical, ecological, and social values. Many of the creative people involved in implementing these new ideas and attitudes will be women. Three green job areas almost guaranteed to grow in the near future are in renewable energy, environmental protection, and green building and energy efficiency.

A major challenge in green technology in the coming decades will be dealing with climate change. This will require many technologists trained in biology and environmental protection.

EDUCATION FOR GREEN CAREERS

Many green technology careers are still considered nontraditional for women. However, these are just the careers that today's young women should consider entering. Most pay more than so-called traditional female jobs such as secretary or teacher. Many have opportunities for advancement even without a college degree, although a degree always helps. The jobs require diverse skills, and there are green jobs that will appeal to almost everyone. Some green jobs are physically demanding, but no more so than jobs such as nursing or waitressing. Finally, green jobs are rewarding. A woman in a green career has the satisfaction of knowing that she is performing a vital service, one that will improve society, the environment, and the planet.

A woman in the renewable energy field might work as a wind turbine service technician, maintaining and repairing huge turbines on wind farms. She might learn these skills on the job or in an apprenticeship program. As the field advances, formal training and certification through a technical school or community college will likely be required. Windmill technicians should be mechanically inclined, physically fit, and comfortable working at great heights. Solar photovoltaic (PV) installers, or solar panel installers, need electrical training and experience in construction, particularly roofing. This can be on-the-job training, apprenticeships, or attendance at technical schools or community colleges. The position requires strong math and problem-solving skills.

A second growth area in the green economy is environmental protection. One example of a position

TARA WEBB: APPRENTICE ELECTRICIAN

After completing a pre-apprenticeship training course for women in trades, Tara Webb earned a certification and obtained her first trade job, as an electric materials handler. A year later, she entered the highly competitive apprenticeship program of the International Brotherhood of Electrical Workers (IBEW) Local 48. On a project employing one hundred people to build seventy windmills, Tara was the only woman. At first, she says, "They weren't sure I was going to be able to do some of the work and climb the towers." She quickly proved herself, climbing three-hundred-foot (ninety-one-meter) towers to wire windmills. Tara believes strongly in protecting the environment and hopes to specialize in green-related work. "If you enjoy using your hands, if you enjoy using your mind, the trades are a wonderful place to be," she says.

in this area is recycling coordinator. This person supervises recycling programs for municipalities or private firms and sometimes educates the public about recycling. A high school education and possibly technical school or community college is appropriate for this position. It requires knowledge of recycling and source reduction practices, plus excellent communication skills.

Many construction-related jobs are available in the third growth area—the field of green building and energy efficiency. A weatherization installer and technician repairs windows, insulates ducts, or performs heating, ventilation, and air-conditioning (HVAC) work to increase a home's energy efficiency. A woman in this position might also perform energy audits for homes or businesses and educate clients on how to increase their building's energy efficiency. After high school, she must obtain certification by

Two workers build a photovoltaic farm by assembling a grid of photovoltaic cells. Such renewable energy projects will provide many opportunities for female technologists in the near future.

completing a training program at a community college or trade school, or by doing an apprenticeship. She must also have construction-related skills; do heavy lifting; work in dirty, cramped spaces; and use hand and power tools safely.

Technologists in green sectors might assist scientists and engineers such as environmental scientists or landscape architects. The pay for entry-level technician jobs is relatively low, but with increasing experience and education, the pay for highly skilled jobs can be substantial. For current pay ranges, consult the U.S. Department of Labor's online *Occupational Outlook Handbook.*

FINDING AND AFFORDING ENVIRONMENTAL TRAINING

Training programs for green jobs are expanding. These may include nonprofit or federally funded training or pre-apprenticeship programs in metropolitan areas, such as the Corps Network, YouthBuild USA, or the U.S. Department of Labor Job Corps. Registered apprenticeship programs through employers or labor unions, for-profit schools with trade programs, community colleges or technical schools, and four-year colleges and universities all provide environmental training. Each candidate must search carefully to find the right program for her interests. After training is completed, certification programs are often available through an employer or independent agency. Licenses are required to practice in certain trades.

The most valuable certifications are those offered by independent agencies. For example, the North American Board of Certified Energy Practitioners certifies solar panel installers.

Women are poised to make a large contribution to the growing field of green technology. Some scholarships and grants specifically for women are available in environmental fields. These are often local, for example, through training providers, civic or religious organizations, women's groups, professional associations, or labor unions. Environmentally oriented girls should definitely take advantage of them.

Chapter five

HEALTH AND BIOTECHNOLOGY: SAVING LIVES THROUGH TECHNOLOGY

iotechnology is the use of biological and bio-chemical processes to produce useful products. It includes everything from using microorganisms to make cheese to developing vaccines, drugs, and genetically engineered crop plants. Of all technology careers, women most often fill those in health and bio-technology. Overall, biological technician jobs will grow by about 10 percent between 2014 and 2022, with the greatest need in biotechnology and medical research. Although jobs in biotechnology are highly competitive, any girl who loves laboratory work in biology, chemistry, or related sciences should be able to find her niche in the biotechnology industry.

GENERAL BIOTECHNOLOGY CAREERS

Many types of scientists and engineers employ technicians and technologists as assistants. They work in university laboratories, private industry, government agencies, or blood banks. A typical example is the medical or clinical laboratory technician, who performs tests on blood, fluids, or body tissues to analyze medical conditions. She uses laboratory equipment and instruments ranging from microscopes to mass spectrometers. Technologists perform more difficult tests and supervise technicians. The job involves routine tasks, such as setting up and maintaining equipment and cleaning glassware, and other more specific tasks, such as preparing and testing samples, compiling data, and keeping records. Experienced technicians and technologists often work closely with scientists in conducting and analyzing experiments. Fields hiring biotechnologists include genetic engineering,

A doctor analyzes readouts from MRI monitor screens. MRI machines are frequently used for diagnosis in biomedical fields. They are operated by highly trained technicians.

epidemiology, forensic science, product development and operations, and quality control.

A technologist working for a biomedical engineer might work with bionic equipment designed to help patients, such as prosthetic limbs, heart valves, or artificial organs. She might use specialized equipment to perform tests such as magnetic resonance imaging (MRI) or computed tomography (CT or CAT) scans. Both tests produce three-dimensional scans of the body, which are clearer and more precise than X-rays and also extremely useful in disease diagnosis. A technologist working for a microbiologist or epidemiologist might study disease-causing bacteria or viruses. An epidemiology technician might use community surveys to understand the spread of a disease. She might help design and carry out experiments to understand disease causes. Strong statistical and observational skills are important in this field.

CAREERS IN GENETIC ENGINEERING

Genetic engineering involves changing the genetic characteristics of an organism by combining DNA from two types of organisms. Independent research in genetic engineering usually requires an advanced degree, often a Ph.D. However, genetic engineering labs also hire lab technicians, who are required to hold only a bachelor's degree. Genetic engineering is vital in medicine, agriculture, and forensic science. Although a technician might use similar techniques and equipment in any lab, the goals of her work might be as diverse as finding a cure for breast cancer, designing a new type of crop plant, or solving a crime.

CHRIS MEDA, CHAMPION OF BIOTECH WOMEN

Chris Meda is the chief business officer at a Menlo Park, California, molecular diagnostics company and chair of the San Francisco chapter of Women in Biotech. She began her career in customer service at a start-up biotechnology company and worked her way up to vice president of sales and marketing. "I took orders over the telephone for a year, with a master's degree," she says. Now, Meda champions the advancement of women into executive positions at biotech companies. However, the process has been slow. In eighteen Bay Area biotech companies, women currently fill only 12 of 129 board positions. "Half the population is women—we should be better represented than this," Meda says. Through the efforts of Meda and others like her, the place for women at the forefront of STEM industries is growing.

Medical technologists (MTs) perform a variety of laboratory tests. In a general laboratory, they might have many duties, including looking for bacteria in bodily fluids, preparing blood for transfusions, or determining concentrations of blood compounds, such as blood glucose. They perform laboratory procedures, interpret results, carry out quality control procedures, and supervise clinical laboratory technicians. They might also interpret test results, conduct experiments, or develop new test methods. In a larger laboratory, an MT might specialize in a single field, for example, analyzing blood samples for bacteria or identifying chromosomal abnormalities.

A cytogenetic technologist studies the genetic basis of diseases. She prepares biological samples (for instance, blood, bone marrow, amniotic fluid, or tumors) and analyzes their chromosomes for the presence of defects. Analysis might involve using highly specialized techniques such as fluorescence in situ hybridization (FISH) or polymerase chain reaction (PCR). A molecular genetic technologist might study DNA to determine cancer risk, diagnose genetic disorders, identify microbial agents, match tissues for possible organ transplantation, identify disaster victims, or determine parentage. These functions also require use of specific genetic

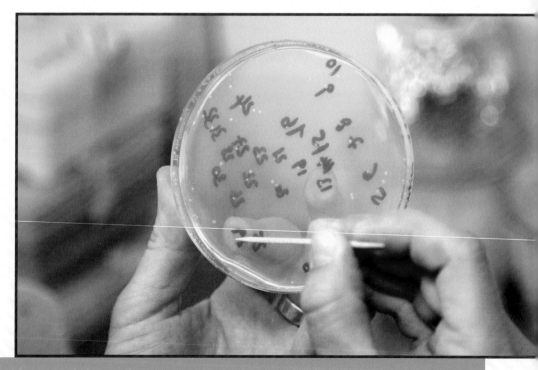

A technician takes samples of genetically modified bacteria, which she will analyze using PCR (polymerase chain reaction). This technique is a standard procedure in biotechnology labs.

techniques, including PCR, gel electrophoresis, and DNA isolation.

CAREERS IN BIOPRODUCTION AND BIOMANUFACTURING

Pharmaceutical companies and biomedical supply houses, among other companies, manufacture thousands of drugs and other biological substances and products, which they then sell to hospitals and to the public. Bioproduction operators are responsible for some aspect of the manufacturing, packaging, and shipping of each product. They follow strict manufacturing protocols, operate machinery, and maintain safety precautions.

Technicians called regulatory QA/QC biomanufacturing specialists carry out quality assurance (QA) or quality control (QC) tests to ensure that each product meets required criteria and specifications before shipping. Both types of technicians are specialized to assist in the production of each of thousands of biological and biomedical products.

PREPARING FOR A BIOTECHNOLOGY CAREER

Although the work done by biological or clinical lab technicians varies, many standard laboratory techniques apply in any lab. For example, every laboratory technician must follow precise standards of cleanliness, safety, and record keeping, as well as specific protocols for each laboratory procedure. She must be able to use

Students learn basic techniques, such as the use of microscopes and other lab equipment, in high school science classes. These are essential background courses for girls planning technology careers.

common types of equipment and glassware and prepare common chemical solutions. Girls can learn these techniques and begin preparing for a biotechnology career by taking high school laboratory courses in biology, chemistry, physics, and mathematics.

Every biotechnologist must have a bachelor's degree. Some schools now offer bachelor's degrees in biotechnology, but many students major in traditional sciences, such as biology, chemistry, biochemistry, or genetics. Since biotechnology is an interdisciplinary field, students should complete a broad range of courses, including organic chemistry, biochemistry, biotechnology, physics, and statistics, as well as required major courses. Certain positions also require certification by a professional organization. Molecular biology technologists are certified by the American Society for Clinical Pathology (ASCP), and molecular genetic technologists by the National Accrediting Agency for Clinical Laboratory Sciences (NAACLS).

Employers usually expect their biotechnologists to have laboratory experience. Experience may come from apprenticeships or from working as a university professor's research assistant. Employers prefer that their hires be able to use computer-based and automated lab equipment, record and analyze data, maintain equipment, and monitor experiments. Biotechnology jobs will show moderate growth and strong competition in the coming decade. Thus, the more laboratory experience a prospective biotechnologist can add to her résumé, the more easily she will find the career she wants.

GRANTS AND SCHOLARSHIPS IN BIOTECHNOLOGY

The popular college-preparatory website School Soup lists scholarships for many specific fields, including biotechnology. These scholarships are from individual universities, government agencies, and biotech-related industries such as Cargill, Inc., Carolina Biological Supply Company, and GlaxoSmithKline (GSK). A number of agencies advertise scholarships and grants for both undergraduate and graduate women. These include the American Association of University Women (AAUW), the

Delta Gamma Foundation's Women in Science grants, and the Maria Mitchell Association's annual Women in Science Award. To locate appropriate scholarships and grants, women and girls should ask school advisers and search the web for opportunities at their college and in their academic field. As with other areas of technology, opportunities for women are available, and women are sought after in the biotechnology field.

Maria Mitchell (1818–1889) was the first professional female astronomer in the United States. Pioneers such as Mitchell opened the doors for women in today's STEM careers.

GETTING YOUR FIRST TECHNOLOGY JOB

F inding that first technology job involves the same basic process as all job searches. It is best carried out as a series of steps. First, successful job hunters begin with a plan, determining the type of job they want and the companies or organizations to approach. Second, every job seeker needs an excellent résumé and cover letter to sell herself to an employer. Third, the job seeker must become comfortable and confident being interviewed. Even with a great résumé and cover letter, a strong interview is essential to "close the deal."

Before, during, and after securing a job, the new technologist should master the art of networking. This is particularly important for women in technology, who are often entering a male-dominated environment. People in the field can provide important tips and help the new hire learn to fit into her new position. Girls can begin early to learn the skills needed to land and hold a job.

Much of the hard work of a job search can be done from home. This includes online research, interview preparation, and the development of résumés and cover letters.

PLANNING A JOB SEARCH

Any young woman looking for a job should first develop a plan. She should consider exactly what it is that she is looking for—what type of job, work-place, or even specific companies or organizations that interest her. She should discuss her job search with professors, career counselors, or others who can help narrow down the best types of jobs. College career planning departments and online job-search sites are extremely helpful. The applicant should learn as much as possible about potential employers by reading websites and asking employees, professors, and others who know the company.

Next, an applicant should list the skills and experience she has to offer an employer. This includes collecting information about education and past jobs, including addresses and phone numbers, to use in filling out applications. She should contact three or more people, preferably teachers or past employers, to serve as professional references. They should be able to judge accurately her experience and ability to perform the jobs. She should ask them if they are willing to be professional references and give each reference a copy of her résumé. She should choose references carefully, based on their willingness to provide glowing recommendations.

WRITING A RÉSUMÉ

The résumé and cover letter provide the prospective employer's first impression of the applicant and must show her to her best advantage. Every résumé contains standard sections: contact information, education, licenses or certificates, work experience (including relevant volunteer work and internships), special skills, and professional memberships. Especially for a first résumé, applicants should carefully study examples online. A first résumé should be only one page long. It should be accurate, neat, easy-to-read, and flawless in spelling and punctuation.

The résumé should highlight the most relevant aspects of a person's skills and experience. A young woman applying for a position with a green energy firm should list all experience—paid and unpaid— relating to green technology, but she should not clutter her résumé with irrelevant work experience. An energy audit done for a school project and summer volunteer work at the local recycling center are more relevant experiences than paid work at a fast-food restaurant. In addition to degrees and diplomas, the education section should list certificates, honors, and awards. Academic honors highlight the applicant's intelligence and hard work. Technology-related awards show excellence in her chosen field.

WRITING A COVER LETTER

The résumé for a first technology job will likely be the same for all employers, but each cover letter should be unique. It should be directed to the specific person in the company who is handling the hiring. The letter should sound professional—clear and factual, but not boastful. It should concentrate on what the applicant has to offer the employer, never on what she wants from them.

The cover letter should be no more than one page long. The first paragraph should briefly explain the applicant's purpose, including the name of the position sought and how she came to hear of it. The second paragraph should then introduce the applicant and list her most relevant skills and experience. It should relate terms from the job announcement to her specific experiences and abilities. The writer should strive to make herself stand out, using examples from past work and successes. She should answer the question: what do I have to offer that is unique among all applicants? A third and final short paragraph should indicate the applicant's willingness to interview for the position and end with a sincere thank you for the reader's consideration. The letter should include complete contact information, including telephone number and e-mail address. The cover letter is usually included in the body of an email, while the résumé is included as an e-mail attachment.

INTERVIEWING

An excellent cover letter and résumé should lead to offers for interviews. This is the applicant's first chance to make a face-to-face impression, and it will ultimately decide whether she gets the job. Thus, careful preparation is vital.

The best preparation is thinking about possible interview questions in advance, preparing answers to them, and practicing with friends. Websites about

TYPICAL INTERVIEW QUESTIONS

Every interview is different, but certain general questions are fairly typical:
- What were your responsibilities at your previous job?
- What was your favorite course in school and why?
- How do you handle stress?
- Why are you interested in this job?
- Why should we hire you over other candidates?
- Tell us about yourself and your interests.
- What is your greatest weakness?

interviewing often have lists of general questions. There will also be questions about the applicant's skills and knowledge related to the specific job, including terminology used in the industry. For a position requiring mechanical or electrical knowledge, interviewers might ask questions on how to analyze or troubleshoot a problem. For a green job, they might ask about the applicant's commitment to green action—for example, whether she recycles or drives an energy-efficient car.

Good interviewing involves common sense. Research the company in advance so you can ask

Good preparation helps a person appear relaxed and confident during an interview. Preparation should include researching the company and practicing answers to likely questions.

one or two specific questions about the job. Dress neatly and appropriately. Be on time—preferably five to ten minutes early. Be pleasant and positive. Have a few copies of your résumé handy for anybody who may sit in on the interview. Bring a list of references as well. After the interview, always send a thank-you note to the interviewers. Several days later, follow up with an e-mail to show continued interest in the position.

NETWORKING

Networking in business is the process of cultivating business-related contacts and friendships that will be helpful in advancing one's career. Networking is a give-and-take activity; each contact must contribute to the relationship. A strong network can help in finding information about potential employers or even landing a new job, although this is not necessarily its main purpose. Networking also helps keep people up-to-date on news and advances within the field.

Network members can come from anywhere—friends and acquaintances, family members, class-mates, social media contacts, coworkers, outside business acquaintances (such as family doctors or lawyers, for example), or people from conferences. Building a network is a slow, ongoing process. Its purpose is not to get an instant job but to build a career through gradually expanding contacts. First impressions are key, so it is always important to put your best foot forward. In the U.S. Department of Labor's 2011 "Why Green Is Your Color: A Woman's Guide to a Sustainable Career" report,

Networking requires attending events and constantly meeting new people. An ever-expanding network of contacts is one way to keep up-to-date on advancements in your career field.

Ellen Telander, who has built a career in recycling, stated, "Get to know the people in the field. Network as much as you can as young as you can... it's all about who you know."

MEETING CHALLENGES AS A FEMALE TECHNOLOGIST

STEM careers are essential to the United States' future global leadership. The Office on Science and Technology Policy and the White House Council on Women and Girls are advocating for women in STEM careers. These lucrative careers help women while also helping the country. Women in STEM careers earn, on average, 33 percent more than women in other careers, and the male-female wage gap is smaller in STEM fields. According to First Lady Michelle Obama, "If we're going to out-innovate and out-educate the rest of the world, we've got to open doors for everyone. We need all hands on deck, and that means clearing hurdles for women and girls as they navigate careers in science, technology, engineering, and math."

WOMEN AS PROFESSIONALS

How does a young woman in a new STEM job make a good impression, fit into her workplace, and rise through the ranks? Nothing makes a better impression

A female mentor in a new job can be a great asset. She can help a new employee fit in, teach new techniques, and give advice on handling workplace situations.

on employers than an employee who always shows professionalism. Professional behavior always includes respect for everyone, whatever their rank. Respect encompasses courteous behavior, honesty, cooperation, prompt responses to requests, and abiding by workplace rules.

Another guideline for a successful career is finding a mentor. This is an older colleague, preferably another woman, who can advise and train the new employee. A mentor serves as a role model, a living example of a successful woman in the tech field. She can provide training on technical aspects of a new job, which may be less stressful than learning new techniques from a man. She can provide valuable advice on navigating the mostly male environment of a STEM workplace. As a young woman becomes more of an expert, she can pay it forward by mentoring a newer employee or a teenage girl with STEM aspirations.

Once she gets the job, a new employee should still continue to build her network. She should be friendly, open to meeting new people, and willing to seek and share information on developing technology trends. This shows her interest and knowledge of the field and makes her more visible when promotions or new jobs become available. In addition, women should be committed to lifelong learning. Technology advances extremely rapidly. Advances that are new during a young woman's college years may be obsolete by the time she graduates. Constant updates through websites, articles, and training courses are essential for women to stay current in STEM fields.

DISCOURAGING GIRLS FROM STEM

Fewer women than men enter STEM careers, and women leave these careers at higher rates. Why does this happen? Lower participation of women in STEM begins in childhood, when many people treat boys and girls differently. A little girl who takes charge is often called "bossy," while a little boy is called a "leader." Leadership is perceived as a good thing while bossiness is considered to be bad. A little boy might more often be called assertive (a positive trait), while a little girl is more likely to be called pushy or aggressive (negative traits). Girls are taught at an early age to fall back and let boys take charge.

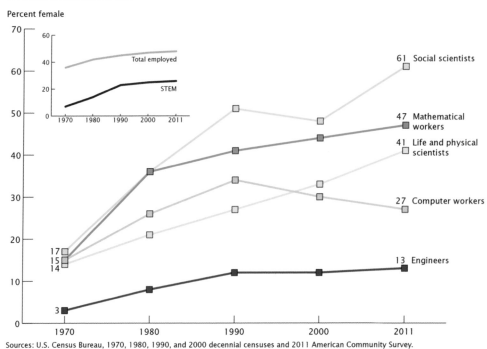

Women's Employment in STEM Occupations: 1970 to 2011
(Data based on sample. For information on confidentiality protection, sampling error, nonsampling error, and definitions, see *www.census.gov/acs/www/*)

Percent female

Sources: U.S. Census Bureau, 1970, 1980, 1990, and 2000 decennial censuses and 2011 American Community Survey.

As of 2010, more women are in the workforce, but growth in STEM careers is slow. Engineers remain unchanged at about 10 percent; computer workers have actually decreased.

Gender stereotypes persist throughout childhood. Little girls' toys more often relate to appearance or domestic life. Boys' toys generally include vehicles, weapons, and construction sets. A March 2014 *New Scientist* article on gender stereotypes and toys stated, "Toys for boys facilitate competition, control, agency, and dominance; those for girls promote cooperation and nurturance." Cultural biases often prevent buying a boy's toy for a girl (or vice versa). But sometimes these stereotypes are overcome. New Jersey mother Lisa Ryder's nine-year-old daughter wanted to be an astronaut, but the only NASA crew T-shirt Ryder could find in the Land's End catalog was in the boys' section. She complained to the company, and Land's End responded by adding science T-shirts for girls.

Linda Kekelis, founder of TechBridge, a California program that expands options for girls in STEM, says many girls avoid STEM education and careers because they lack self-confidence. Also, girls often have fewer opportunities. Kekelis says, "We hear from our girls that their brothers get the Legos and that the computer is in their brother's bedroom." Mostly boys go to robotics camps, she also says. Her colleague Erica Wong adds that there are few women or minority role models of scientists and engineers.

Research shows that, even when girls and boys perform equally in mathematics, girls have less confidence in their math abilities. They hold themselves to a higher standard than boys do and choose not to enter math-intensive fields for fear of failure. Differences in self-confidence begin as early as elementary and middle school and increase throughout high school and college. Many parents and teachers often reinforce low self-confidence. They encourage girls less, evaluate them differently than boys, and give them lower recommendations. Thus, even interested girls avoid pursuing STEM activities and, later, STEM careers. Meg Urry, chair of the physics department at Yale University, states, "I'm afraid all the evidence points to obstacles and discouragement for women going into

STEM fields in the U.S." But, she adds, this means the problem can be solved by removing the obstacles and substituting encouragement.

Girls themselves can counter these statistics simply by standing up for themselves. They can ask for STEM-related toys and opportunities. A girl who wants a Lego set rather than a dollhouse can and should say so. She can explain her interests to her parents and ask for their support. She can seek out teachers and adult friends who will give her opportunities to practice technology. She can take math and science courses, ask for help when necessary, and persist even when she is the only girl in the class. She can learn to defend and explain her interests to other boys and girls, rather than apologizing or giving up. Just by "doing her own thing," a young girl can show that girls are just as capable of using technology or excelling in STEM areas as boys.

GENDER DISCRIMINATION IN THE WORKPLACE

Even after overcoming gender biases in childhood, young women may still encounter obstacles in their STEM careers. Gender discrimination is any situation in which a woman is treated less favorably than a man. In the workplace, discrimination occurs in pay, advancement, and an employer's handling of family matters such as pregnancy and child care. In the worst cases, it may involve sexual harassment, in which a woman is intimidated, insulted, or humiliated because of her gender. Repeated sexual harassment results in a hostile workplace.

FIGHTING GENDER DISCRIMINATION LEGALLY

Women can address gender discrimination through legal means. Ingrid was a machine operator at a bottling plant. When she became pregnant, her doctor told her not to lift more than twenty pounds (nine kilograms). She asked her supervisor to be temporarily relieved of this job requirement. He refused but offered to transfer her to a lower-paying job. Ingrid filed an Equal Employment Opportunity Commission (EEOC) charge of sex discrimination. An investigation revealed that the supervisor had previously reassigned the lifting duties of a man with an injured arm and a woman with a hernia. Ingrid won her suit because the supervisor had discriminated based on her pregnancy—a form of sexual discrimination.

Within STEM fields, part of the pay gap is a result of women's choices of majors. Fewer women choose degrees in physics, computer science, and engineering—the areas with the highest pay. Even within specific STEM fields, women still make significantly less than their male counterparts. In 2011, the average female engineering technician made 43,000 dollars, while the average male at the same level made 56,000 dollars. Once women are in the field, they advance more slowly than men, and often, their careers stall before they reach the highest positions.

Sometimes women fail to advance because of issues surrounding pregnancy and child care.

Approximately 85 percent of women will become pregnant during their working lives. Yet often employers do not ensure these women's ability to keep their jobs and perform them safely. They may even fire or demote a woman after her child is born. Other women leave positions due to inflexible work demands. In addition, the mother is more often the parent who misses work when a child is ill. Even if lost workdays do not affect her ability to do her job, a woman may be given lower performance evaluations and bypassed for promotions.

OVERCOMING GENDER DISCRIMINATION

While women should definitely be aware of gender discrimination issues, they should also realize this is not the normal workplace situation. People are becoming more aware of gender discrimination, and workplaces are developing codes of conduct to address it. A woman can approach gender discrimination (including sexual harassment) by preparing in advance and deciding how to deal with various situations. This includes discussing potential problems with mentors, discussing ongoing issues with supervisors, and if necessary, seeking legal remedies. To overcome gender discrimination, women must learn to stand up for themselves, support other female coworkers, and actively work to replace workplace gender discrimination with gender-neutral policies.

Women in STEM careers still face some of the same gender-based prejudices faced by "almost astronauts" such as Jerrie Cobb. But recognition of women's underrepresentation in STEM careers and

Women in New York City protest gender pay discrimination on Equal Pay Day, April 8, 2014. At that time, women earned only seventy-seven cents for every dollar earned by men.

the development of programs to improve their participation ensure the coming generation of women will be better accepted in the workplace than past generations. Today's women are diving into complex technological careers and proving their worth. They are learning to navigate STEM workplaces with pride and self-confidence. They are better prepared to overcome obstacles and take their place as equal contributors to our country's technological culture. In the process, they are making the technology workplace even more inviting for their own daughters and granddaughters—the tech girls of tomorrow.

Glossary

APPLIED SCIENCE Type of science that uses known scientific principles or concepts to solve specific problems; includes engineering and technology.

BIOTECHNOLOGY Use of biological or biochemical processes to produce useful products.

COMMUNICATION TECHNOLOGY (OR TELECOMMUNICATION) Technology that facilitates communication between individuals or groups not present in the same location, including telephone, telegraph, cable, radio, television, video, e-mail, and electronic data transmission.

COVER LETTER Letter sent with a résumé when applying for a job that introduces the applicant and provides additional information.

EPIDEMIOLOGY Branch of medical science that studies the spread and control of disease in a population.

GENDER DISCRIMINATION A situation in which a woman or group of women are treated less favorably than others, for example, in the workplace.

GENETIC ENGINEERING Changing the genetic characteristics of an organism by combining DNA from two types of organisms.

GREEN JOBS Jobs that produce goods or services that benefit the environment, conserve natural resources, or make production processes more environmentally friendly.

GREEN TECHNOLOGY Methods and materials involved in living without destroying or damaging Earth or its organisms and resources, and without overexploiting its resources.

MENTORING Advising or training a younger colleague.

NETWORKING Cultivating business-related contacts and friendships to advance one's career.

PROFESSIONALISM Behavior in the workplace that follows an accepted code of conduct, including showing respect for everyone, honesty, cooperation, and abiding by workplace rules.

PURE SCIENCE Type of science that works on solving problems having no immediate real-world application but may be later adapted to one.

RENEWABLE ENERGY Energy obtained from a source that is not depleted when used, such as wind or solar; non–fossil fuel energy.

RÉSUMÉ Brief summary of personal, educational, and professional qualifications; used when applying for a job.

SEXUAL HARASSMENT Situation in which a person is made to feel intimidated, insulted, or humiliated due to his or her sex or gender; harassment can be either verbal or physical.

STEM CAREER Any career within the fields of science, technology, engineering, or mathematics.

SUSTAINABILITY Using resources to provide for this generation's needs without compromising the resources needed for coming generations.

TECHNOLOGY The practical application of knowledge, or the application of knowledge to the practical aims of human life or manipulation of the human environment.

National Alliance for Partnerships in Equity (NAPE)
91 Newport Pike, Suite 302
Gap, PA 17527
(717) 407-5118
Website: http://www.napequity.org
The NAPE website titled "Stem Careers: Just for Students" provides statistics and information on reasons students should study STEM fields and opportunities for careers in these areas. It includes some resources specifically oriented toward young women.

Society for Canadian Women in Science and Technology (SCWIST)
#311–525 Seymour Street
Vancouver, BC V6B 3H7
Canada
(604) 893-8657
Website: http://www.scwist.ca
This nonprofit organization promotes and encourages Canadian women in STEM fields.

The White House Office of Science and Technology Policy (OSTP)
Eisenhower Executive Office Building
1650 Pennsylvania Avenue
Washington, DC 20504
(202) 456-4444
Website: http://www.whitehouse.gov/administration /eop/ostp
The OSTP publishes reports and fact sheets and highlights recent news items relating to its "Women in

STEM" initiative, sponsored jointly by the OSTP and the White House Council on Women and Girls.

Women in Communications and Technology
116 Lisgar Street, Suite 300
Ottawa, ON K2P 0C2
Canada
(800) 361-2978
Website: https://www.wct-fct.com
This nonprofit organization for women who work in communications and technology helps create jobs and advance women in the field through networking, leadership and skills development, and mentoring.

Women in Technology (WIT)
10378 Democracy Lane, Suite A
Fairfax, VA 22030
(703) 766-1153
Website: http://www.womenintechnology.org
WIT is a nonprofit organization that seeks to advance women in the field of technology, from the classroom to the boardroom.

WEBSITES

Because of the changing nature of Internet links, Rosen Publishing has developed an online list of websites related to the subject of this book. This site is updated regularly. Please use this link to access the list:

http://www.rosenlinks.com/TECH/Tech

For Further Reading

Brown, Jordan D. *Robo World: The Story of Robot Designer Cynthia Breazeal* (Women's Adventures in Science). Danbury, CT: Children's Press, 2005.

Etingoff, Kim. *Women in Chemistry* (Major Women in Science). Broomall, PA: Mason Crest, 2013.

Etingoff, Kim. *Women Who Built Our Scientific Foundations* (Major Women in Science). Broomall, PA: Mason Crest, 2013.

Farmer, Lesley. *Teen Girls and Technology. What's the Problem, What's the Solution?* New York, NY: Teacher's College Press, Columbia University, 2008.

Gibson, Karen Bush. *Women of Space: 23 Stories of First Flights, Scientific Missions, and Gravity-Breaking Adventures* (Women of Action). Chicago, IL: Chicago Review Press, 2014.

Grayson, Robert, and Tracy Deutsch (contributor). *Estée Lauder: Businesswoman and Cosmetics Pioneer* (Essential Lives). Minneapolis, MN: ABDO Publishing, 2013.

Indovino, Shaina. *Women in the Environmental Sciences* (Major Women in Science). Broomall, PA: Mason Crest, 2013.

Indovino, Shaina. *Women in Information Technology* (Major Women in Science). Broomall, PA: Mason Crest, 2013.

Indovino, Shaina. *Women Inventors* (Major Women in Science). Broomall, PA: Mason Crest, 2013.

Indovino, Shaina. *Women in Physics* (Major Women in Science). Broomall, PA: Mason Crest, 2013.

Indovino, Shaina. *Women in Space* (Major Women in Science). Broomall, PA: Mason Crest, 2013.

Karnes, Frances A., and Kristen R. Stephens. *Young Women of Achievement: A Resource for Girls in Science, Math, and Technology.* Amherst, NY: Prometheus Books, 2002.

Kiernan, Denise. *The Girls of Atomic City: The Untold Story of the Women Who Helped Win World War II.* New York, NY: Touchstone Books, 2014.

Lewis, Anna M. *Women of Steel and Stone: 22 Inspirational Architects, Engineers, and Landscape Designers* (Women of Action). Chicago, IL: Chicago Review Press, 2014.

Morgan, George D. *Rocket Girl: The Story of Mary Sherman Morgan, America's First Female Rocket Scientist.* Amherst, NY: Prometheus Books, 2013.

Stone, Tanya Lee. *Almost Astronauts: 13 Women Who Dared to Dream.* Somerville, MA: Candlewick Press, 2009.

Tiscareno-Sato, Graciela. *Latinnovating: Green American Jobs and the Latinos Creating Them.* Hayward, CA: Gracefully Global Group, 2011.

Welty, Tara. *Jane Goodall* (Conservation Heroes). New York, NY: Chelsea House Publications, 2011.

Yount, Lisa. *Rosalind Franklin: Photographing Biomolecules* (Trailblazers in Science and Technology). New York, NY: Chelsea House Publishing, 2011.

Bibliography

Ball State University. "Careers in Telecommunications." 2014. Retrieved September 23, 2014 (http://cms.bsu.edu/academics/collegesanddepartments/telecommunications/lifeafterbsu/careers).

Bonar, Samantha. "Study: Women Don't Choose STEM Careers Despite Their Skills." Tech Page One. May 13, 2013. Retrieved October 6, 2014 (http://techpageone.dell.com/business/study-women-stem-careers/#.VDLwsRauTXM).

GEN. "Top Ten Biotech Jobs Most in Demand Over the Next Decade." Genetic Engineering & Biotechnology News, August 4, 2012. Retrieved October 17, 2014 (http://www.genengnews.com/insight-and-intelligence/top-ten-biotech-jobs-most-in-demand-over-the-next-decade/77899666).

Goudarzi, Sara. "Top 10 Emerging Environmental Technologies." LiveScience, April 19, 2007. Retrieved October 13, 2014 (http://www.livescience.com/11334-top-10-emerging-environmental-technologies.html).

Graham, Brad. "Why Is STEM Still a Four-Letter Word for Women? Seven Leaders Weigh In." Huff Post Impact, July 21, 2014. Retrieved September 15, 2014 (http://www.huffingtonpost.com/ravishly/why-is-stem-still-a-four-letter-word-for-women_b_5606306.html).

Hill, Catherine, Ph.D., Christianne Corbett, and Andresse St. Rose, ed. *Why So Few? Women in Science, Technology, Engineering, and Mathematics.* Washington, DC: AAUW, 2010.

Huhman, Heather R. "STEM Fields and the Gender

Gap: Where Are the Women?" *Forbes*, June 20, 2012. Retrieved October 23, 2014 (http://www .forbes.com/sites/work-in-progress/2012/06/ 20/stem-fields-and-the-gender-gap-where-are -the-women).

I Seek Careers. "Women in Science, Technology, Engineering, and Math (STEM)." Retrieved September 15, 2014 (http://www.iseek.org/ careers/womenstem.html).

St. Rose, Andresse. "STEM Major Choice and the Gender Pay Gap." On Campus with Women, Association of American Colleges and Universities. Spring 2010. Retrieved October 23, 2014 (http:// archive.aacu.org/ocww/volume39_1/feature. cfm?section=1).

United States Department of Labor. Why Green Is Your Color. *A Woman's Guide to a Sustainable Career.* Women's Bureau. Retrieved October 13, 2014 (http://www.dol.gov/wb/Green_Jobs_ Guide/GreenJobs%20Final_11.2011.pdf).

US News & World Report. "Best Technology Jobs." 2014. Retrieved August 23, 2014 (http://mon-ey.usnews.com/careers/best-jobs/rankings/ best-technology-jobs).

Wetfeet. "Industry Overview: Aerospace and De-fense." December 3, 2012. Retrieved October 3, 2014 (https://www.wetfeet.com/articles/indus-try-overview-aerospace-and-defense).

White, Mary Gormandy. "Careers in Space Sci-ence." LoveToKnow Jobs & Careers. Retrieved October 6, 2014 (http://jobs.lovetoknow.com/Ca-reers_in_Space_Science).

Index

ABOUT THE AUTHOR

Carol Hand has a Ph.D. in zoology with a specialization in marine ecology. She has taught college, worked for standardized testing companies, developed multimedia science and technology curricula, and written more than twenty science and technology books for young people. Having both university and workplace experience in science and technology, she has firsthand understanding of the challenges women face in the STEM workplace.

PHOTO CREDITS

Cover © iStockphoto.com/pixdeluxe; cover and interior pages background image © iStockphoto.com/cosmin4000; cover and interior pages text banners © iStockphoto.com/slav; pp. 5, 24 © AP Images; p. 9 © iStockphoto.com/appleuzr; p. 12 © iStockphoto.com/LL28; p. 15 © iStockphoto.com/Andrew Rich; p. 17 ChameleonsEye/Shutterstock.com; p. 20 © iStockphoto.com/shironosov; p. 27 Andrey Armyagov/Shutterstock.com; p. 28 Orlando Sentinel/Tribune News Service/Getty Images; p. 31 Gilles Bassignac/Gamma-Rapho/Getty Images; p. 36 Gabriel Kuchta/isifa/Getty Images; p. 38 U.S. Department of Labor Women's Bureau, "Why Green Is Your Color: A Woman's Guide to a Sustainable Career," p. 2 photo; p. 41 Pedro Castellano/E+/Getty Images; p. 45 Medioimages/Photodisc/Digital Vision/Thinkstock; p. 48 alohaspirit/E+/Getty Images; p. 50 Hasloo Group Production Studio/Shutterstock.com; p. 52 NYPL/Science Source/Getty Images; p. 54 Inti St Clair/Blend Images/Getty Images; p. 58 Africa Studio/Shutterstock.com; p. 60 Klaus Vedfelt/Iconica/Getty Images; p. 62 lightpoet/Shutterstock.com; p. 64 U.S. Census Bureau, Disparities in STEM Employment by Sex, Race, and Hispanic Origin, 2013; Richard B. Levine/Newscom.

Designer: Nicole Russo